DECONSTRUCTING POWERFUL SPEECHES

TECUMSEH
SPEECH AT VINCENNES

REBECCA SJONGER

CRABTREE
PUBLISHING COMPANY
WWW.CRABTREEBOOKS.COM

CRABTREE
PUBLISHING COMPANY
WWW.CRABTREEBOOKS.COM

Author:
  Rebecca Sjonger
Series research and development:
  Janine Deschenes and Ellen Rodger
Editorial director:
  Kathy Middleton
Editor:
  Ellen Rodger
Proofreader:
  Wendy Scavuzzo
Graphic design:
  Katherine Berti
Image research:
  Rebecca Sjonger and Katherine Berti
Print and production coordinator:
  Katherine Berti

Images:
Andy Thomas, Tecumseh and the
  Osage: p. 24–25
Getty Images
  Bettmann: p. 42
Granger: p. 22, 35
  Sarin Images: p. 10 (top right)
Indiana Historical Society: p. 3,
  8 (center right)
Internet Archive; Open Library;
  Memoirs of a Captivity Among the
  Indians of North America From
  Childhood to the Age of Nineteen:
  p. 24
Library of Congress: p. 1, 23
Penn Museum, Courtesy of,
  image #152428 and #240881:
  p. 30 (top right)
Shutterstock
  arindambanerjee: p. 40
  Everett Historical: p. 4 (bottom)
  Gilbert Stuart: p. 27 (bottom)
  Sean Pavone: p. 9 (top)
  tanuha2001: p. 42–43 (bottom)
  Thomas Sully: p. 27 (top)
Toronto Public Library: front cover,
  p. 15
University of Texas Libraries,
  The University of Texas at Austin:
  p. 5 (bottom right)
Wikimedia Commons
  Baskin, Forster and Company,
  Chicago: p. 26
  Charles Bird King: p. 6 (left)

Chris Light: p. 6 (right),
  10 (bottom left)
David F. Barry, Photographer,
  Bismarck, Dakota Territory: p. 28–29
Edward H. Latham: p. 33
Elliot Schwartz for StudioEIS:
  p. 20 (top)
Emmet Collection of Manuscripts
  Etc. Relating to American History,
  Scan by NYPL: p. 20 (bottom)
Engraving by John Simon, after Jan
  Verelst: p. 20 (center bottom)
H. A. Brooks. June 1916:
  p. 8–9 (bottom)
Hulton Archive: p. 30–31
James Lambdin; The White House
  Historical Association: p. 39 (top)
John Reuben Chapin: p. 36–37
Missouri History Museum: p. 38
National Portrait Gallery,
  Smithsonian Institution, Rembrandt
  Peale (1778–1860): p. 7 (top right)
Nyttend: p. 7 (bottom)
Owen Staples: p. 10 (top left)
Popular Graphic Arts: p. 39 (bottom)
Rosser1954 Roger Griffith: p. 5
  (inset top left)
United States Department of the
  Interior: p. 9 (center right)
William & Mary Digital Archive: p. 9
  (center left)
All other images by Shutterstock

Library and Archives Canada Cataloguing in Publication

Sjonger, Rebecca, author
    Tecumseh : speech at Vincennes / Rebecca Sjonger.

(Deconstructing powerful speeches)
Includes bibliographical references and index.
Issued in print and electronic formats.
ISBN 978-0-7787-5242-4 (hardcover).--
ISBN 978-0-7787-5256-1 (softcover).--
ISBN 978-1-4271-2185-1 (HTML)

    1. Tecumseh, Shawnee Chief, 1768-1813--Juvenile literature.
2. Speeches, addresses, etc., American--Indian authors--Juvenile
literature. 3. Indians of North America--Civil rights--United States-
-History--Juvenile literature. 4. Indian activists--United States--
Biography--Juvenile literature. 5. Shawnee Indians--Biography--
Juvenile literature. I. Title.

E99.S35T26 2019   323.1197   C2018-905571-5
                                           C2018-905572-3

Library of Congress Cataloging-in-Publication Data

Names: Sjonger, Rebecca, author.
Title: Tecumseh : speech at Vincennes / Rebecca Sjonger.
Description: New York, New York : Crabtree Publishing, [2019] |
  Series: Deconstructing Powerful Speeches | Includes bibliographical
  references and index.
Identifiers: LCCN 2018050344 (print) | LCCN 2018059538 (ebook) |
  ISBN 9781427121851 (Electronic) |
  ISBN 9780778752424 (hardcover : alk. paper) |
  ISBN 9780778752561 (pbk. : alk. paper)
Subjects: LCSH: Tecumseh, Shawnee Chief, 1768-1813. Speech
  to Governor Harrison--Juvenile literature. | Indians--Kings and
  rulers--Juvenile literature. | Shawnee Indians--Land tenure--Juvenile
  literature. | Indians of North America--Northwest, Old--Government
  relations--1789-1869--Juvenile literature. | Harrison, William Henry,
  1773-1841--Juvenile literature. | Northwest, Old--History--1775-
  1865--Juvenile literature. | Speeches, addresses, etc., Indian--Juvenile
  literature. | Oratory--Juvenile literature.
Classification: LCC E99.S35 (ebook) | LCC E99.S35 S56 2019 (print) |
  DDC 977.004/973170092--dc23
LC record available at https://lccn.loc.gov/2018050344

Crabtree Publishing Company

www.crabtreebooks.com   1-800-387-7650

Printed in the U.S.A./012019/CG20181123

**Published
in Canada
Crabtree Publishing**
616 Welland Ave.
St. Catharines, Ontario
L2M 5V6

**Published in the
United States
Crabtree Publishing**
PMB 59051
350 Fifth Avenue, 59th Floor
New York, New York 10118

**Published in the
United Kingdom
Crabtree Publishing**
Maritime House
Basin Road North, Hove
BN41 1WR

**Published
in Australia
Crabtree Publishing**
3 Charles Street
Coburg North
VIC 3058

CONTENTS

INTRODUCTION

PADDLES ON THE RIVER

The news spread quickly when Shawnee warriors were spotted on the Wabash River in summer 1810. They traveled in dozens of **dugout canoes**. When the group stopped at an American fort, an officer noted they looked ready for battle. They were heading toward Vincennes. At the time, it was the **capital** of the Indiana Territory. The **governor**, William Henry Harrison, was expecting them. He had asked to meet in a council with their leader, Tecumseh.

At the age of 42, Tecumseh was on his way to becoming a legend. He was a member of the Kispoko part of the Shawnee nation. When he was born around 1768, his parents gave him a name that may have meant "shooting star." It could also have referred to a panther crossing the sky. This would honor a great panther his family's **clan** believed in. As a boy, Tecumseh lived in the area around what is now Springfield, Ohio. His family taught him the traditions of their clan. He learned to fish and hunt alongside the other boys. Tecumseh also became skilled at making weapons. He trained to be a warrior just like his father, Pukeshinwau.

A Shawnee warrior as depicted in a European illustration of the 1800s

4

Pictures of Tecumseh are based on a French trader's sketch of him.

TIMELINE

1500s	French traders arrive on the continent
1600s	British colonization begins
1763	Britain's Royal Proclamation creates "Indian Reserve"
1768	Tecumseh born
1775–1783	American Revolution
1800	August, Indiana Territory created
1810	Tecumseh and Governor Harrison meet at Vincennes
1813	October 5, Tecumseh dies
1816	State of Indiana forms
1841	March 4, Harrison becomes president of the United States
1841	April 4, President Harrison dies

SETTLER CRUSH

The Shawnee were just one of many Indigenous nations who lived in what would become North America. They all faced a common enemy. People arriving from Europe were settling on their lands. This disrupted their ways of life. In 1763, the British tried to solve the problem. They set aside a territory west of the Appalachian Mountains. It was meant solely for Indigenous peoples. Settlers kept moving onto the land, however.

When Tecumseh was six, his father left to fight settlers in the Ohio Valley. Pukeshinwau never returned home. He was killed in the Battle of Point Pleasant. The American Revolution began soon after. When Britain lost this war to the Americans in 1783, things grew even worse for the Shawnee and other nations. Land agreements made with the British colonies became worthless. They had a new nation to deal with.

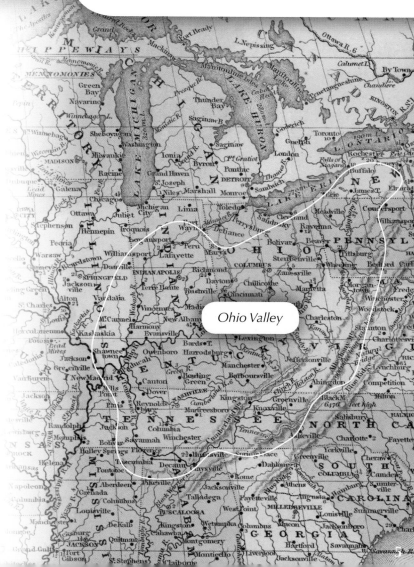

Ohio Valley

TECUMSEH'S GOALS

Cheeseekau was Tecumseh's older brother. He showed a teenaged Tecumseh how to wage war against the settlers. Cheeseekau was killed in a conflict with settlers when Tecumseh was in his early twenties. His grief did not stop the young warrior from fighting. Over the years, he earned a place as a leader because of his successes in battle.

Tecumseh also had a younger brother. Tenskwatawa became a Shawnee leader too. Some people called him the Prophet. He taught that the settlers were the children of an evil spirit. Tecumseh and his brother had a plan. They wanted Indigenous peoples to form a confederacy, or a group of **allies**.

Its aim would be to save their territories and traditional ways of life. The brothers pushed old enemies to join together. They tried to unify nations living from the Great Lakes region to the Mississippi Valley. Their headquarters was a village nicknamed "Prophetstown" on the Tippecanoe River.

Tecumseh had two goals when he headed to Vincennes. He planned to argue that Governor Harrison could not buy land from any one group. Tecumseh believed the land belonged to all the nations. He also wanted to convince the Indigenous peoples who were selling their land to join his confederacy. He felt that, together, they could resist the American takeover.

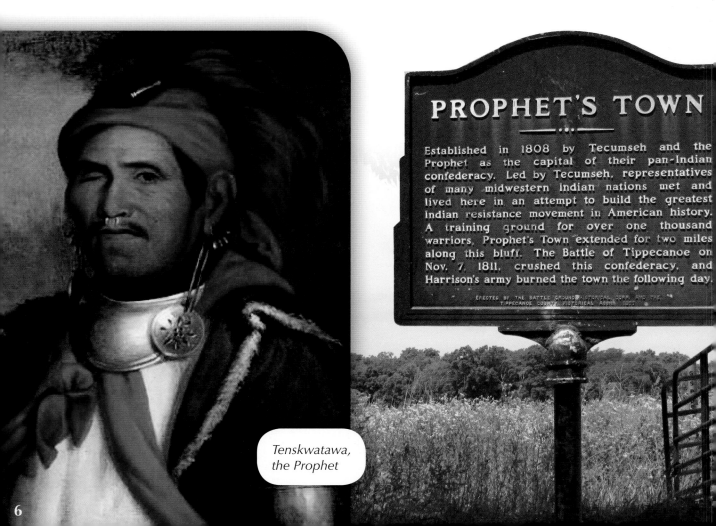

Tenskwatawa, the Prophet

PROPHET'S TOWN

Established in 1808 by Tecumseh and the Prophet as the capital of their pan-Indian confederacy. Led by Tecumseh, representatives of many midwestern Indian nations met and lived here in an attempt to build the greatest Indian resistance movement in American history. A training ground for over one thousand warriors, Prophet's Town extended for two miles along this bluff. The Battle of Tippecanoe on Nov. 7, 1811, crushed this confederacy, and Harrison's army burned the town the following day.

ERECTED BY THE BATTLE GROUND HISTORICAL CORP. AND THE TIPPECANOE COUNTY HISTORICAL ASSN. 1970

Tecumseh met Harrison on August 20 at Grouseland. This was the governor's red brick mansion in Vincennes. One story claims that Tecumseh was offered a chair on a platform where the governor sat. The Shawnee leader chose to sit on the grass instead. He wanted to be closer to the earth. The two men's points of view were as different as their choice of seating. The mood in the audience was charged as they waited to see what would happen. On one side were people who had lived on the land for thousands of years. On the other side were settlers forming a new country—on that same land. Tecumseh's speech would highlight the growing **hostility** between them.

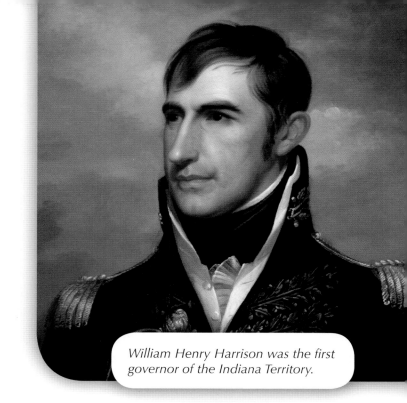

William Henry Harrison was the first governor of the Indiana Territory.

Harrison's house in Vincennes, Indiana

Tours of Grouseland
Begin at the Front Door
of the Mansion

CHAPTER 1

PERSUASIVE PRIMARY SOURCES

Tecumseh's speech at Vincennes is a primary source. The **United States Library of Congress** calls these resources "the raw materials of history." They are original, firsthand accounts. These sources include text, audio files, and images. Letters, video recordings, and photos are just a few examples. **Data** in a birth certificate, an opinion poll, and other recorded facts are also primary sources. They bring us as close as we can get to being at a certain time in history. Through his speech, Tecumseh gives us a view of life in the late 1700s and early 1800s.

WIDENING THE VIEW

Some materials are created after an event or time period. Often, they come many years later. These are secondary sources. Another way to describe them is an interpretation, which is a kind of explanation. They **analyze**, or study, one or more primary sources, as well as other secondary sources. They may also express an opinion. These sources include textbooks used in schools, music reviews, and magazine articles. They can explore an event or issue in many ways. This provides a richer view of the past. These resources also give context, which is useful background information. This book is a secondary source focused on the speech Tecumseh gave at Vincennes.

Tecumseh's speech to Governor William Henry Harrison, Vincennes

Tecumseh foresaw a future in which Indigenous peoples would increasingly be forced from their traditional lands.

The U.S. Library of Congress is the world's largest library. It holds a huge collection of primary sources.

A letter written by William Henry Harrison in 1834 in which he gives an account of what he knows of the death of Tecumseh.

Tecumseh fought against the sale and loss of Indigenous lands to North American settlers.

FACT CHECK

Finding a few key details is the first step in analyzing a primary source. Checking these facts helps determine how useful and relevant the source is.

Maker, such as a writer

Intended audience

Date it was created

AUGUST 20, 1810

Purpose

Place it was made

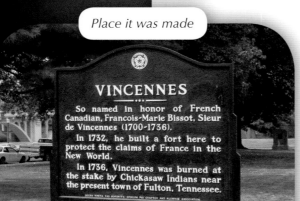

VINCENNES

So named in honor of French Canadian, Francois-Marie Bissot, Sieur de Vincennes (1700-1736).

In 1732, he built a fort here to protect the claims of France in the New World.

In 1736, Vincennes was burned at the stake by Chickasaw Indians near the present town of Fulton, Tennessee.

Maker's point of view

WRITTEN RECORDS

In the past, speeches were recorded by hand. They were written as the words were spoken, or later from memory. A transcript is a printed version of a primary source. Transcripts, such as the one below of Tecumseh's speech, may be the only form available to study. In 1810, the person writing out this speech may have used a feather quill and pot of ink. In the full transcript, Tecumseh introduces himself, naming his tribe and acknowledging his forefathers so that listeners would know who he was and where his knowledge and authority come from.

Speaker: *Tecumseh*
Audience: *Governor Harrison*
Date: *August 20, 1810*

> *Tecumseh's speech to Governor Harrison 20th Aug. 1810*
>
> *Brother:*
>
> *It has been the object of both myself and brother from the beginning to prevent the lands being sold…*

The title of this handwritten transcript from the Indiana Historical Society shows the maker of the speech, the intended audience, and the date it was given. Tecumseh did not refer to the date or use Harrison's name in the speech itself.

Tecumseh also spoke to the Indigenous groups at the council. This included leaders from the Wea and Piankeshaw nations.

Tecumseh states the purpose of his speech. He likely had a second goal, too. Learn more about it starting on page 16.

READ IT

Check out the Indiana Historical Society's copy of the full transcript of Tecumseh's speech at **https://bit.ly/2kVS43F**

FILLING IN THE GAPS

The details needed to assess a primary source are not always easy to find. The source itself may not mention them. For example, the setting of Vincennes is not in the transcript of Tecumseh's speech. Libraries and museums collect as many facts as they can about their resources. They are listed in catalogs, or databases. This information is often useful when studying a speech.

LANGUAGE BARRIERS

Tecumseh spoke the Shawnee language. He needed someone to **interpret** his speeches into other languages. Joseph Barron interpreted Tecumseh's speech at Vincennes. Barron was a French trader who spoke many languages. He would listen to Tecumseh speak. Then Barron would explain what was said in his own words for the American audience. He also interpreted for the Indigenous people who did not know the Shawnee language.

A GAME OF BROKEN TELEPHONE

Tecumseh's speeches have much to offer as primary sources. However, the use of non-Indigenous interpreters and transcribers limits them. What Tecumseh said is probably different from the speech we have to study today. This may have been done on purpose or by accident. The same is true of many historical sources.

WHAT'S THE POINT?

The spoken word can be a powerful tool to promote change. Speeches such as Tecumseh's usually present an argument about one issue. They use persuasive language to share the speaker's point of view. The words are crafted to sway an audience to think a certain way.

DIGGING DEEPER

Speeches are products of their time. Tecumseh may have used language such as "my red children." How do you think today's readers should respond?

Reading silently is a very different experience than hearing someone say the words.

MAKING AN ARGUMENT

CLAIM

Speeches support their arguments with claims, which are statements or conclusions.

Playing a sport is good for you.

EVIDENCE

Evidence is data or facts that prove the claims are true.

Many studies show that playing a sport improves physical and mental fitness.

WARRANT

Warrants connect claims and evidence to support a course of action.

Overall fitness leads to a long, happy life, so we should all play a sport.

APPEAL

Appeals in speeches urge the audience to act.

If you do not yet play a sport, you should start today!

RHETORICAL LANGUAGE

The art of persuasion used in speeches and other texts is called rhetoric. Rhetorical language uses three main strategies to sway the audience.

LOGOS

Logos asks the audience to consider logic, or reason. In a speech, logos may begin with a general idea that is then supported by facts. It could also use these facts as a starting point to draw conclusions.

Playing a sport strengthens bones and muscles. It makes good sense for you to play a sport.

ETHOS

Ethos urges the audience to believe the speaker because of his or her trustworthy character. This may be done by sharing personal experiences, finding common ground, or showing respect.

As someone who has coached for twenty years, I advise playing a sport. Then you can experience the benefits for yourself.

PATHOS

Pathos plays on the audience's emotions to win them over.

Not playing a sport could harm your health in the long run. You might regret it for the rest of your life.

Students can use rhetorical language to strengthen the claims, evidence, and warrants in their speeches.

WORDS THAT WORK

Every speech uses rhetorical language in its own ways. It is supported by rhetorical devices, such as:

- Comparing two things that are not alike in an **analogy**
- Using figurative language, such as **metaphors** and **similes**
- Exaggerating in **hyperboles**
- Giving things human qualities through **personification**
- Repeating key words and phrases
- Making some facts sound less important than they really are

A color sketch of Tecumseh taken from an early wood engraving by Benson Lossing. Lossing copied an earlier sketch done by a fur trader who had met Tecumseh. One of the difficulties with early sketches is that the artist may not have met the subject, which is why so many images of Tecumseh look different.

LOST INFORMATION

It is impossible to know which of these devices Tecumseh used in his speech at Vincennes. His original Shawnee wording is lost to us. It does appear that Tecumseh relied on repetition, though. He used it to highlight important points in his speech.

THE POWER OF VOICE

Voice affects the delivery of a speech. The way someone pronounces and produces the sounds in words changes the ways audiences hear them. This is called diction. It also includes the words a speaker or writer chooses to use. Changing the tone in which words are said can also transform the message. Imagine the phrase "Thanks a lot" said in a friendly way or with anger. The rising and falling rhythms of those tones is called cadence. Along with emphasis, all these things help speakers make their points.

LOST TO HISTORY

No audio recordings of Tecumseh's speech means an important way of studying it is not available. However, secondary sources describe witnesses who claimed to have heard Tecumseh give speeches. They suggest he spoke with great power and passion.

HEARD NOT READ

Speeches are unique arguments because the writers intend them to be heard. Arguments that are delivered aloud can mix language with voice. The same words can be presented with very different effects, depending on the speaker's voice. The experience is not the same when a speech is read silently instead.

15

CHAPTER 2

WORDS AND MEANING

We can deconstruct, or **critically analyze**, a speech for language and hidden meanings. Tecumseh's speech at Vincennes contains the parts of an argument and rhetorical language described in the last chapter. His other speeches and writings also show how he used these tools. They all help reveal a picture of Tecumseh's struggle against settler ideas and culture.

ORDERING IDEAS

At the start of Tecumseh's speech, he describes the French traders. He then moves on to the British. Finally, he refers to the Americans. This way of arranging information is sequential. It presents ideas or events in order. They could also be shown comparatively. This method compares and contrasts information. For example, Tecumseh describes the similarities and differences among these groups. Speeches may also present ideas causally. This is cause and effect. The argument is made by describing the reasons behind events, then the results.

PURPOSE

The reason for making a speech is its purpose. Governor Harrison had made treaties, or agreements, to buy land from some Indigenous groups. Tecumseh's central argument was that they did not have the right to sell the land. Some secondary sources suggest the Shawnee leader had another goal for this speech. He challenged Indigenous people who made deals with the Americans. He appealed to them to join his confederacy instead, in the belief that a strong, united Indigenous group could negotiate with the Americans as equals.

DECONSTRUCT IT

To find claims and evidence in a speech, ask:
- What conclusions are being made?
- Which facts or data support these statements?
- Is the speaker using their voice, such as with emphasis or pacing, to reinforce any text?

Speaker: *Tecumseh*
Audience: *Governor Harrison*
Date: *August 20, 1810*

> *You recollect that the **time** the **Delaware** lived near the white **people** (**Americans**) and satisfied with the promises of **friendship** and remained in security, yet one of their towns was surprised, and the men, women and children **murdered**…Since the peace was made you have killed some of the Shawanoes, Winebagoes, Delawares, and Miamies, and you have **taken our lands from us**, and I do not see how **we can remain at peace with you**… you said if we could show that the land was sold by persons that had no right to sell, **you would restore it**. Those that did sell did not own it, it was **me**… Every thing I have said to you is the truth. The **Great Spirit** has **inspired me**…*

In 1782
An Indigenous nation
In the village of Gnadenhutten, Ohio
The transcriber may have added this to clarify which "white people" Tecumseh meant
From settlers
Almost 100 people were killed by American forces
Through unfair treaties and by force
Tecumseh makes this conclusion after supporting it with multiple examples
Tecumseh likely knows this will not happen but states it as a claim
"Me" is underlined in the transcript, so Tecumseh may have emphasized what he sees as a fact
The Indigenous creator of the universe; earlier, Tecumseh referred to Harrison's God, so this could also be a challenge not to make light of his beliefs
Tecumseh may have considered this to be evidence

SPEAKER SPOTLIGHT

In some versions of Tecumseh's speech, he is said to have declared:

> *...unite in claiming a common and equal right in the land... it never was divided but belongs to all... Sell a country! Why not sell the air, the great sea, as well as the earth?*

This famous Tecumseh quotation may have been taken from a letter to Harrison. It was sent around the same time as the council in Vincennes. These words sum up his arguments to the governor and the groups who sold their land.

CLAIMS AND EVIDENCE

Tecumseh supported his arguments with claims. Then he backed up these conclusions with facts. The kinds of claims and evidence used are affected by factors such as the audience, setting, and time period. It is unlikely, for example, that Tecumseh used the same details at a council with Americans as he used at an Indigenous council. In 1810, accurate data would be difficult to find. Tecumseh drew on facts that he believed to be true.

DECONSTRUCT IT

When listening to or reading a speech, ask:
- What is the speaker's central argument?
- Who is the speaker appealing to?

Speaker: *Tecumseh*
Audience:
Governor Harrison
Date: *August 20, 1810*

> *...**you** wish to prevent the **Indians**...to unite and let them consider their land as the common property...If you continue to purchase of **them**, it will produce **war among the different Tribes**...they had **no right to the claim they set up**...It has been the **object** of both myself and **brother**...to prevent the lands being sold...*

The American government

A common term in this time period, as was "Tribes"

Traditional Indigenous territories

A warning to Americans as well as to Indigenous peoples who were in the audience

The nations who sold land to the United States

Tecumseh believed these territories were owned by all Indigenous peoples

Purpose

Tenskwatawa, the Prophet

19

SPEAKER SPOTLIGHT

Tecumseh's other speeches use claims and evidence too. In this one, delivered sometime between 1811 and 1813, he spoke about the disappearance of Indigenous nations. He used it as evidence to support his claim that the settlers would destroy them.

Pequot

*...Where today are the **Pequot**? Where are the **Narragansett**, the **Mohican**, the **Pokanoket**...? They have **vanished** before the **avarice** and the **oppression** of the **White Man**...Will we let ourselves be destroyed in our turn without a struggle, give up...our country **bequeathed** to us by the Great Spirit...?*

Tecumseh used repetition as he listed Indigenous nations from the eastern parts of the continent

They were killed or moved off their land

Greed

Ongoing unjust treatment

The transcriber may have capitalized these words because Tecumseh emphasized them or it may have been the writer's own style

His call to resist the settlers

Like the peoples he mentioned earlier

Given

Tecumseh considered it a fact that the land was given to them by a higher power

Narragansett

Mohican

DIGGING DEEPER

There are no audio records of Tecumseh's speech. It is impossible to know for sure how he used diction or tone. How do you think he may have used his voice to sway the audience?

Pokanoket

WARRANTS AND APPEALS

Appeals in speeches request action of some kind. Tecumseh appealed to Governor Harris to stop the land sales. The Shawnee leader also urged other Indigenous leaders to unite with him. Warrants are statements that justify a course of action. Tecumseh linked his claims and evidence to explain why they should join his **confederacy**.

DECONSTRUCT IT

Find warrants and appeals in a speech by asking:
- Is the speaker urging the audience to act or think a certain way?
- How are claims and evidence being connected to convince them?

> *Speaker:* Tecumseh
> *Audience:* Governor Harrison
> *Date:* August 20, 1810

*…we would still be your friends… you want by your **distinctions of Indian Tribes**…to make them to **war with each other**…This land that was sold and the goods that was given for it, was only done **by a few**… The Treaty at Fort Wayne was made through the threats of Winemac, but in future we are **prepared to punish** those chiefs who may come forward to propose to sell their land…*

Tecumseh appeals for unity
Governor Harrison
Treating them differently
Tecumseh accused Harrison of creating conflicts
Chiefs from the Delaware, Eel River, Miami, and Potawatomi nations who were not in Tecumseh's confederacy
Warning to everyone at the council

EXPANDING THE MEANING

Tecumseh speaks of how almost 3 million acres (121.4 million hectares) of land in the southern part of the Indiana Territory was sold for about $5,000 worth of everyday items and weapons. He emphasizes that this was an unjust sale because only a few benefited. He notes that while the 1809 Fort Wayne treaty was one of hundreds of land agreements made between Indigenous people and the U.S. government, it was made through only one leader, the Potawatomi leader Winemac, and not all.

DIGGING DEEPER

What evidence can you find in Tecumseh's speech that reveals the time period in which it was written?

SPEAKER SPOTLIGHT

Tecumseh carried on the traditions of earlier leaders. They often spoke for a political purpose. Governor Harrison noted that Tecumseh seemed to have been influenced by Pontiac. He was a famous Odawa (Ottawa) warrior. Pontiac led a confederacy of nations against the British. In 1763, he spoke at a council of Indigenous nations. His warrants and appeals echoed in Tecumseh's speeches decades later.

Speaker: Chief Pontiac
Audience: Indigenous council gathered at Detroit
Date: 1763

> *It is important for us, my **brothers**, that we **exterminate** from our **lands** this **nation**…You see as well as I that **we can no longer supply our needs**, as we have done from **our brothers, the French**…we must all **swear their destruction**…*

Warriors were men
Destroy an unwanted population
Traditional Indigenous territories around the Great Lakes
The enemy at the time was Britain—the war for American independence began eight years later
Indigenous ways of life were disrupted
These pro-French feelings were passed down to Tecumseh
They must destroy or be destroyed themselves

Pontiac's resistance led to a three-year-long conflict known as Pontiac's War.

RHETORICAL LANGUAGE

Making speeches and **debating** were important skills in Tecumseh's culture. Leaders needed to command people's attention. They had to call them into action. Tecumseh's speech blended Indigenous customs with Western ideas. For example, he called the audience "brothers." But he also spoke of the nations as one united people, just like the American states. This was uncommon for Indigenous leaders to do. He referred to himself as the "head" of the nations. This was another borrowed **concept**. Tecumseh used logos as he asked Governor Harrison to be reasonable. Pathos is seen in his emotional appeals.

DECONSTRUCT IT

To identify rhetorical language in a speech, ask:
- How is the speaker using logic and reason to persuade the audience?
- Does the speaker's character help support the central argument?
- How is the audience being swayed by emotion?

Speaker: *Tecumseh*
Audience: *Governor Harrison*
Date: *August 20, 1810*

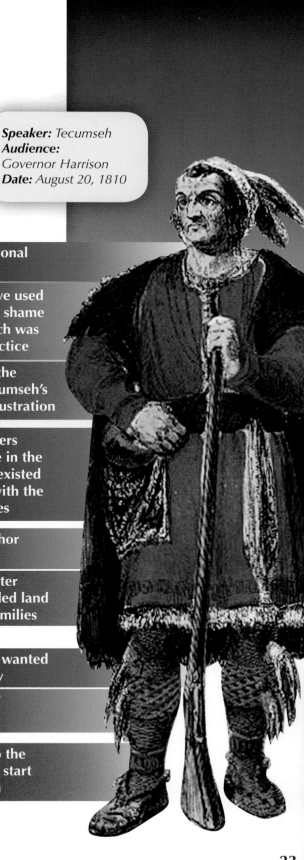

> *I wish you to listen to me well…as I think you do not clearly understand what I before said to you. I shall explain it again. When we were first discovered it was by the French, who told us that they would adopt us as their children…The next father we found was the British… we then found new fathers in the Americans…I want now to remind you of the promises of the white people… The Great Spirit has inspired me…*

Begins with traditional invitation to listen

Tecumseh may have used a sarcastic tone to shame the governor, which was an Indigenous practice

Repetition shows the importance of Tecumseh's purpose and his frustration

Trappers and traders came from France in the early 1600s, and existed mostly at peace with the Indigenous peoples

A common metaphor in this speech

They came in greater numbers and needed land to support their families

The latest settlers wanted the whole country

Indigenous way of declaring intent

Custom to refer to the Great Spirit at the start or end of a speech

SPEAKER SPOTLIGHT

Tecumseh used pathos to stir up the audience's emotions in his address to the Osage nation in Oklahoma around 1812. John Dunn Hunter was a settler who claimed to be a captive of the Kickapoo. He wrote down this speech from his memories of the day.

John Dunn Hunter

Speaker: *Tecumseh*
Audience: *Osage nation*
Date: *1812*

> …*we **must assist each other to bear our burdens**…The white people came among us **feeble**; and now **we have made them strong**, they wish to kill us…**as they would wolves and panthers**…nothing will satisfy them but the whole of our **hunting grounds, from the rising to the setting sun**… My people are brave and numerous; but **the white people are too strong for them alone**. I wish you to **take up the tomahawk** with them. If we all unite, we will **cause the rivers to stain the great waters with their blood**… The Great Spirit is angry with our enemies; he speaks in thunder, and the earth swallows up villages, and drinks up the Mississippi…*

Emphasizes unity of Indigenous nations
Unable to survive on their own
Indigenous peoples helped settlers learn to live off the land
Americans treated them like wild animals
Land on which to make towns and farms
Indigenous use of nature imagery to describe a time period
Tecumseh would not have admitted this to an American audience
Go to war; Indigenous weapon
Appealed to warriors who have trained their whole lives for battle
Custom to link the natural and supernatural

ONE OF MANY GREAT SPEAKERS

Tecumseh's talent as a speaker surprised the Americans. They thought he was unique among the Indigenous peoples. This revealed one of their biases, which are one-sided, unfair beliefs. In fact, the Shawnee leader came from a rich **oral tradition**. He was used to telling stories and passing on ideas by talking to a group. Tecumseh used the skills he gained as part of his culture to present his point of view at Vincennes.

DIGGING DEEPER

Bias prevents people from respecting people or things they are not familiar with. Can you think of any examples of bias in your own life?

Speaking, retelling history, and sharing stories are a part of Indigenous oral tradition. Tecumseh's Osage audience would have understood how to listen as well as share.

CHAPTER 3

ANALYZING PERSPECTIVES

A primary source usually reveals the maker's point of view or **perspective**. This is how someone feels about an issue. When the source is a speech, the maker and the speaker are not always the same person. Sometimes, a writer creates a speech on behalf of the person who gives it. The writer aims to present the speaker's perspective, though. In Tecumseh's case, the use of a non-Indigenous interpreter means we cannot be sure exactly which words he said. His perspective is clear, however.

HISTORICAL VIEWPOINTS

Tecumseh's perspective was influenced by his time period. The same is true of the perspectives of his audience. The way people think and act today is different from when Tecumseh delivered his speech at Vincennes. It shines a light on his era in American history.

The Americans at Vincennes were building a new country. They viewed the land as empty and something to take, or something that could be bought or traded.

DECONSTRUCT IT

To examine a speaker's perspective, ask:
- How does the language used show the speaker's feelings?
- How could the speaker's point of view be summed up in one sentence?

Speaker: Tecumseh
Audience: Governor Harrison
Date: August 20, 1810

President Jackson made dozens of land treaties with Indigenous nations.

James Madison was the president of the United States from 1809 to 1817.

> *Flags were given to **them**…hold up your flags and **no harm will be done you**…the consequence was, that the person bearing the flag was **murdered**… can you blame me for placing little confidence in the **promises** of our father the Americans… Perhaps it is by direction of the **President** to make those **distinctions**… **we do not like it**… If you do not restore the land, **you will have a hand in killing them**…*

The Shawnee

They would show peace had been made with the settlers

Using this word highlights that the death was an illegal act

Including land treaties

President James Madison was respectfully called "Great Chief" or "Great Father" in many Indigenous speeches, so this may show how Tecumseh felt about him

Divisions between nations

Tecumseh made his perspective clear

Tecumseh used pathos and strong language as he referred to the chiefs who made the land deals, some of whom were in the audience

SPEAKER SPOTLIGHT

Indigenous nations did not all view **land claims** in the same way. This is shown in the different ways Tecumseh shared his point of view. In 1811, he argued that the Choctaw and Chickasaw nations must resist the Americans. He urged them to awaken from their "false security and **delusive** hopes." It seems they did not share Tecumseh's view of the threat to their lives. His plea to change their minds is emotional and raw.

CAREFULLY CHOSEN WORDS

Perspective is also seen in **nuanced** language. Using a certain word can help create a feeling that sways the audience. For example, Tecumseh referred to Governor Harrison as "Brother" instead of using his official title. Careful word choices may have been changed as Joseph Barron interpreted Tecumseh's speech. The loss of nuance is not the only problem with the interpretation. Barron may have added his own perspective into the speech. A careless mistake in the written transcript could also affect what we see as Tecumseh's point of view.

Speaker: *Tecumseh*
Audience: *Choctaw and Chickasaw nations*
Date: *1811*

> "The **annihilation of our race** is at hand unless we unite in **one common cause** against the **common foe**... Your people, too, will soon be as falling leaves and scattering clouds before their blighting breath. You, too, will be driven away from your native land and ancient domains **as leaves are driven before the wintry storms**...Our **broad domains** are fast escaping from our grasp..."

Total destruction	
Tecumseh put together many nations into one group for his political purposes. American settlers also came from many backgrounds but were seen as one group.	
The confederacy's resistance	
Americans	
Used natural imagery and pathos	
Large traditional territories	

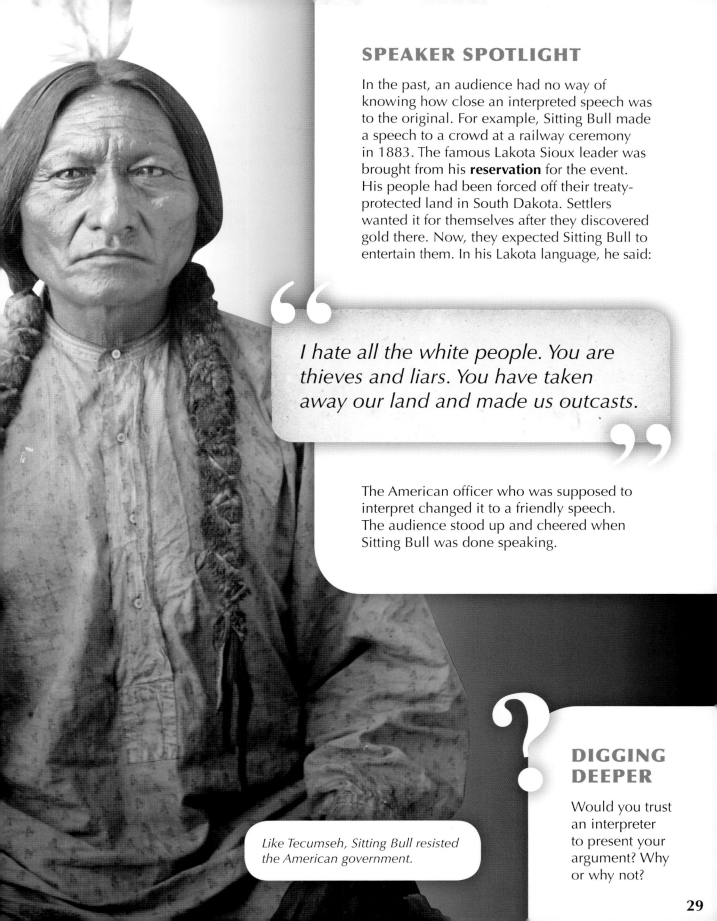

SPEAKER SPOTLIGHT

In the past, an audience had no way of knowing how close an interpreted speech was to the original. For example, Sitting Bull made a speech to a crowd at a railway ceremony in 1883. The famous Lakota Sioux leader was brought from his **reservation** for the event. His people had been forced off their treaty-protected land in South Dakota. Settlers wanted it for themselves after they discovered gold there. Now, they expected Sitting Bull to entertain them. In his Lakota language, he said:

> *I hate all the white people. You are thieves and liars. You have taken away our land and made us outcasts.*

The American officer who was supposed to interpret changed it to a friendly speech. The audience stood up and cheered when Sitting Bull was done speaking.

Like Tecumseh, Sitting Bull resisted the American government.

DIGGING DEEPER

Would you trust an interpreter to present your argument? Why or why not?

MISSING INFORMATION

Speeches rarely share more than one perspective. This means they can be rich sources of historical perspectives when they are deconstructed. Makers of speeches choose what information to share and how to present it. They also decide what to leave out. This may include details that weaken their claims. Tecumseh's speech at Vincennes uses the information that works well for his own purposes.

DECONSTRUCT IT

To uncover what may be missing from a speech, ask:
- What are the possible limitations in this primary source?
- Are any facts left out or presented unfairly?
- What other sources could be investigated?

Shawnee clothing decorated with beadwork. On wampum belts, the beadwork recorded history.

Speaker: *Tecumseh*
Audience: *Governor Harrison*
Date: *August 20, 1810*

> *…The next father we found was the British…They never troubled us for our land…let the traders come among us. Then perhaps some of our young men will occasionally call on you to get their guns repaired…it is the sentiments of all the red people that listen to me…*

They formed the first thirteen colonies

Tecumseh ignores bad deals such as Britain's purchase of present-day Kentucky and western Pennsylvania from the Six Nations Confederacy in 1768. This led to the loss of Shawnee territory.

Tecumseh chose not to include that they would be warriors

He does not point out that the guns could then be aimed at Americans

Tecumseh refers to Indigenous unity throughout his speech. However, Winnebagos and Kickapoos had fought to the death that summer—and they were part of the confederacy. Clearly, not everyone was united.

EXPAND THE VIEW

Much can be learned by looking at more than one side of an argument. Studying other speeches or writings can show what is missing from a speech. They could be from the same time period or later. Sometimes, they are in response to the speech. Secondary sources often look at many perspectives to provide a deeper understanding of the issue.

DIGGING DEEPER

What might influence the perspectives in a personal diary and in a biography written about the same person?

Tecumseh recalled the trading relationships Indigenous peoples had with the French, British, and Americans to emphasize areas of cooperation.

PLANS FOR A NEW COUNTRY

The American government wanted as much land as it could get. This would help the United States grow larger. President Andrew Jackson's perspective was shaped by his role as the leader of a new country. His feelings come through in his second annual message. This kind of speech given by an American president is now known as the State of the Union address. Jackson delivered it to the government on December 6, 1830.

Speaker: President Andrew Jackson
Audience: Government
Date: December 6, 1830

> "…the **benevolent policy** of the Government, steadily pursued for nearly **30 years**, in relation to the removal of the **Indians** beyond the white settlements is approaching to a **happy consummation**…It will…**free them from the power of the States**; enable them to **pursue happiness**…under their own **rude institutions**; will **retard**… **lessening their numbers**, and perhaps cause them… to cast off their savage habits and **become an interesting, civilized, and Christian community**…What good man would prefer a country covered with forests and ranged by a **few thousand savages** to our extensive Republic, studded with cities, towns, and prosperous farms…?"

Annotation
Charitable or kind
Plan to force Indigenous peoples off their lands
During Tecumseh's lifetime
Almost 2,000 words of this speech focused on "Indians"
Nearing its goal
This never happened
The Declaration of Independence called "the pursuit of happiness" a right of the people
Refers to Indigenous traditions that offended Americans
Slow
Millions of Indigenous people lived in what is now the United States before the arrival of Christopher Columbus in 1492. Wars and newly introduced diseases dropped that number to about 600,000 in 1800. Only about 250,000 Indigenous people lived there by the late 1800s
American perspective that *assimilation* was desirable because it meant adopting settler culture, government, and ways of life, which he suggests any "good man" would consider superior
Note the incorrect low number and language of the time period

READ IT

To see the full text of President Andrew Jackson's second annual message address, visit **https://to.pbs.org/2MbYNSN**

LOSING THE WILL TO FIGHT

Many Indigenous groups shared Tecumseh's perspective at first. However, as the United States grew in power, it became more difficult and deadly to openly **resist**. Chief Joseph was a leader in the Nez Perce nation. In 1877, about 800 of his people refused to move onto a reservation. Instead, they fled their home in Oregon. They tried to escape to Canada. On October 5, 1877, they surrendered to the U.S. Army in Montana. Defeated, Joseph shared his point of view:

Speaker: *Chief Joseph*
Audience: *Nez Perce nation*
Date: *October 5, 1877*

Chief Joseph also used an interpreter when speaking with Americans.

> *I am **tired of fighting**. Our chiefs are killed…The old men are all dead…It is cold and we have no blankets. The little children are freezing to death…My heart is sick and sad. From where the sun now stands, I will **fight no more forever**.*

American soldiers hunted the Nez Perce as they walked over 1,100 miles (1,770 km)
Four leaders were killed in battles along the way
At least 145 people died on the 106-day journey
They left their homes in early summer and the weather had changed by the beginning of October
Some people claimed his death by heart failure in 1904 was the result of his broken heart
Indigenous telling of time
Unlike Tecumseh, Joseph would no longer resist the Americans

WISHING THEM WELL

A historical sign in Tuscaloosa, Alabama, displays another perspective. It shows where Yoholo Micco, a leader from the Muscogee nation, addressed the state government in 1836. He gave his speech in the Muscogee language. The transcript in *The Huntsville Democrat* is a translation. His friendly words are unexpected. Some secondary sources suspect the tone used may have delivered a less kind message. However, the newspaper reports that some in the audience were moved to tears. Their response does not make sense if the voice used was not heartfelt.

Speaker:
Yoholo Micco, Muscogee leader
Audience:
Muscogee nation
Date: *1836*

> I come here, **brothers**, to see the **great house of Alabama** and the **men who make the laws,** and to say farewell in **brotherly kindness** before I go to the far West…In time gone by, I have thought that the **white men** wanted to bring burden and ache of heart among my people in driving them from their homes…But I have now become satisfied that they are not unfriendly toward us, but that **they wish us well**…In these lands of Alabama, which have belonged to my forefathers and where their bones lie buried, I see that the Indian fires are going out. Soon they will be **cold. New fires are lighting in the West** for us, **they** say, and **we will go there**. I do not believe our **Great Father** means to harm his **red children**, but that he wishes us well…

brothers	Like Tecumseh, he acknowledges relationships
great house of Alabama	State government building
men who make the laws	Members of the government
to see / farewell	The leader's perspective on the event
go to the far West	The Muscogee were forced to leave their land and take a journey that would become known as the Trail of Tears because so many people died along the way
white men	American settlers
they wish us well	The opposite of Tecumseh's perspective
New fires are lighting in the West	Traditional rhetoric
homes	Homes on reservations
they / we will go there	Americans
Great Father	More than 100,000 Indigenous people were forced onto a territory across the Mississippi River
Great Father	President Jackson
red children	Language of the time period

CHANGING PERSPECTIVES

Readers of a historical speech bring their own perspectives to it. Every analysis is colored by a particular point of view. There are many different ways of looking at Tecumseh's speech at Vincennes, for example. Often, the way a speech is viewed reflects the attitudes of the time in history. As the culture keeps changing, people may view Tecumseh's speech differently.

The **Indian Removal Act** pushed Indigenous peoples off their land and led to the Trail of Tears.

CHAPTER 4

INFLUENCES THEN AND NOW

Tecumseh spoke for about two hours at Vincennes. This included the time it took to interpret his words. From the transcript, it seems that Governor Harrison started speaking next. Some sources claim he asked Tecumseh why there were so many Indigenous languages if the Great Spirit wanted them to be one nation. Tecumseh became very angry. He called the governor a liar. Shawnee warriors held up their weapons and Harrison pulled out his sword. To avoid a fight, the governor quickly ended the council.

FINAL WORDS

Tecumseh was unhappy that he had not met his goals. The Shawnee leader returned to Vincennes the next day. He apologized for acting in anger. He also spoke to Harrison about President Madison. Tecumseh said:

> " *I hope the Great Spirit will put some sense into his head and induce him to direct you to give up this land…He will not be injured by the war…you and I will have to fight it out.* "

AN UNCOMMON GENIUS

Tecumseh's speech did not convince Harrison to cancel any land deals. The Indigenous nations in the audience did not rush to join the confederacy. However, the governor was impressed by Tecumseh. Harrison warned the U.S. War Department about the Shawnee leader. Harrison called Tecumseh a genius. The governor believed that in the right setting, Tecumseh could upset "the established order of things."

Illustrations of the events at Vincennes are often depicted from the government perspective. Harrison feared the power of Tecumseh's rhetoric and ideas.

PROPHETSTOWN DESTROYED

Tecumseh kept trying to unite the Indigenous nations. He was traveling when Governor Harrison led hundreds of soldiers to Prophetstown on November 6, 1811. Harrison and Tenskwatawa agreed to meet and talk the next day. Instead, the confederacy's warriors attacked in the morning. When they ran out of ammunition, the Americans overcame them. Tenskwatawa and his people fled from the Tippecanoe River area. The governor's men burned the village to the ground.

DIGGING DEEPER

If the intended audience was not swayed by an argument, do you think that means the speech was a failure? Why or why not?

Tecumseh's dream of a united Indigenous territory died with him on the battlefield.

TECUMSEH'S LAST BATTLE

The United States declared war on Britain in spring 1812. The British promised to create a territory for the Shawnee if they joined the fight. Tecumseh led his soldiers to help Britain's army. His men were outnumbered in the Battle of the Thames in Ontario. The great leader was shot. Tecumseh died on the battlefield on October 5, 1813. Despite his heroic efforts, the British did not keep their promise of support and a territory.

HARRISON FOR PRESIDENT

A few years after Tecumseh died, Indiana joined the union. The American people rewarded Harrison for his defeat of the confederacy. They elected him president. On March 4, 1841, President Harrison gave the longest inaugural, or opening, address in history. He spoke for almost two hours outdoors on a cold winter day. The new president caught pneumonia and died just one month later.

President Harrison's inauguration

William Henry Harrison used the nickname "Tippecanoe" during his campaign for president. It reminded people of his success in crushing Tecumseh's confederacy and in securing Indigenous lands for settlers.

CHANGING HISTORY

Many stories about Tecumseh have been told over the years. The truth in each one is that he influenced history. He said "the only way to stop this evil is for the red people to unite in claiming a common and equal right to the land, as it was at first." Tecumseh did not change the course of events with his speech at Vincennes. However, his efforts made him a hero to many Indigenous peoples.

Today, different nations often work together to push for rights. Non-Indigenous people are learning more about Indigenous perspectives and paying more attention to the harms done in the past and how this influences the present and the future. Old views about land agreements and ownership are shifting. A wider audience is developing an awareness and understanding of the views Tecumseh made in his speech at Vincennes.

*Indigenous protesters in Toronto, Canada, at a **solidarity** rally with the Standing Rock and Cheyenne River Sioux tribes in North Dakota and South Dakota. Those tribes are opposing an oil pipeline near their lands that they fear will poison their water and destroy their **sacred** sites.*

READ IT

To read the full text of Alicia Elliott's piece in *The Globe and Mail*, visit **https://tgam.ca/2qx2dJO**

HOPE FOR THE FUTURE

Female Indigenous writers did not have a place in the newspapers of Tecumseh's time. That is not true today. Alicia Elliott is from the Tuscarora nation. In a national paper in 2018, she shared her perspective on the relationship between Canada and Indigenous peoples. Like Tecumseh, she hopes for a future in which they regain what has been taken from them.

Speaker: *Alicia Elliott*
Audience: *Canadians*
Date: *January 5, 2018*

> *A memo to Canada: Indigenous people are not your incompetent* **children**…*the Canadian government* **continually prevents us** *from creating meaningful change…like every decision* **Canada** *makes about us, without us, we're supposed to smile and accept these arrangements… regardless of how it* **affects our families and our lives**…*Canada's approach to Indigenous people has always been* **akin** *to that of a* **paternal** *head of house in a* **fifties sitcom:** **Father** *knows best…There is an alarming tendency to consider 634 distinct Indigenous nations as one* **homogeneous group**…*Canada has continually failed its* **treaty obligation** *to respect Indigenous nations' right to* **steer our own canoes**…*But we will get there.*

Compare the title to Tecumseh's speech, in which he said things such as "treat us as their children" and "look on us as their children"	
Repeatedly	
Written more than 200 years after Tecumseh said, "you wish to prevent the Indians…"	
Also applies to the United States	
No change from Tecumseh's time or perspective	
Like	
Fatherly	
Typical 1950s funny television show	
They have dealt with French, British, American, and now, Canadian "fathers"	
Identical or the same	
Contrast with Tecumseh's vision of a united group	
Commitments made in historical agreements	
Make their own decisions and choose their own path	

THE FUTURE OF SPEECHES

Perspectives are not the only things that change over time. Tecumseh had to travel in person to Vincennes to deliver his speech. His would have many more options if he was alive today. People can make speeches on a variety of social media channels. They can post videos or speak live to an audience around the world. However, the features of a great speech remain the same. Well-chosen words are still powerful and persuasive.

Russell Means was an Indigenous activist and leader from the Oglala Lakota Sioux Nation. In his well-known 1997 address to the U.S. Senate Special Committee on Indian Affairs, Means greeted the committee in the same way Tecumseh greeted those at Vincennes. "This is the only way we present ourselves to one another that is acceptable. We tell you who we are, where we are from, who we are from, our clans, and we do this without ever saying our name. Anything less would be an insult to you and to my people."